Really Short Walks
Exmoor and Brendon

Robert Hesketh

Bossiney Books

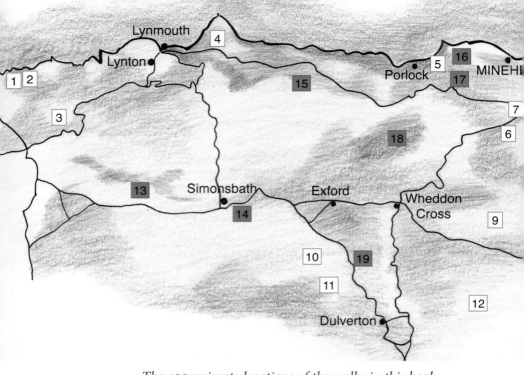

The approximate locations of the walks in this book.
Numbers on green squares indicate there-and-back walks.
All the others are 'circular'.

First published 2012 by
Bossiney Books Ltd, 33 Queens Drive, Ilkley, LS29 9QW
www.bossineybooks.com

© 2012 Robert Hesketh All rights reserved
ISBN 978-1-906474-35-5

Acknowledgements
The maps are by Graham Hallowell.
The cover is based on a design by Heards Design Partnership.
All photographs are by the author.

Printed in Great Britain by R Booth Ltd, Penryn, Cornwall

Introduction

The routes in this book are chosen to show Exmoor's beautiful land and seascapes. All are short, mostly 3-5km (2-3 miles) in length. Whilst some are easy, others are a bit more challenging, so the time needed to complete them will vary. But why hurry? There are many wonderful viewpoints and places of interest to linger over on the way and every walk has its individual character.

Clothing and footwear

Walking Exmoor is a pleasure throughout the seasons so long as you're prepared. Always carry extra layers of clothing as well as a waterproof. Exmoor's weather can change rapidly, and even within a short walk there may be a considerable temperature difference when you climb from a sheltered valley to a breezy hill or cliff top.

On some paths there may be gorse or nettles, so bare legs can be a liability. There will be some mud at most times of the year and perhaps a lot of mud and puddles in winter and after a wet spell. Ideally, therefore, wear walking boots – and certainly not sandals! Wellington boots are not recommended, as they don't 'breathe' or provide ankle support.

Extras

Take drinking water with you, as you will soon need it: dehydration causes tiredness. I recommend taking a walking pole or stick too and a mobile phone if you have one. The sketch maps in this book are just that – sketches. You may want to carry the OS Explorer map, sheet OL9, for extra information.

The countryside

Walking is safe and healthy exercise, but please watch out for uneven ground, rabbit holes, etc.

Despite many pressures on their livelihoods, farmers are still trying to make a living from the land you will pass through. Please respect their crops. Leave gates closed or open as you find them, and keep dogs under control, especially during the lambing and bird nesting seasons.

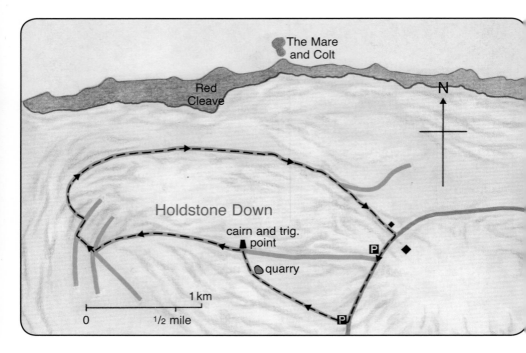

Walk 1 Holdstone Hill

Distance: 3.8 km (2 1/2 miles)

Character: The modest effort of climbing heather-clad Holdstone Hill is rewarded with magnificent views in all directions. Most impressive are Exmoor's massive whale-backed cliffs. Across the Bristol Channel is a long vista of the Welsh coast with the Brecon Beacons behind. Inland, the rolling green hills of North Devon with their chequerboard pattern of hedges stretch on to the Dartmoor horizon.

Please attend to directions as animals have created several additional tracks over Holdstone Down.

Start from the signed car park at SS 624474. Take the unsigned path at the rear. Follow this steadily uphill past a disued quarry to the triangulation pillar and cairn on the summit (349 m).

Take the unsigned path west and downhill with Great Hangman in front of you. At 318 m, with a cliff face of 248 m, Great Hangman is the highest cliff in southern Britain. Reaching

Looking east towards Heddon's Mouth (top photo) and west towards Great Hangman (lower photo)

a junction where five paths meet, bear right and continue downhill to a T-junction of paths.

Turn right, COASTPATH. Bear left at the Coastpath arrow when the path appears to fork at an animal track. Continue on the Coastpath as it veers right (east). When the Coastpath divides, fork right and walk uphill towards two buildings.

Reaching the tarmac lane, turn right and follow it past the entrance to a second small parking area and back to the start.

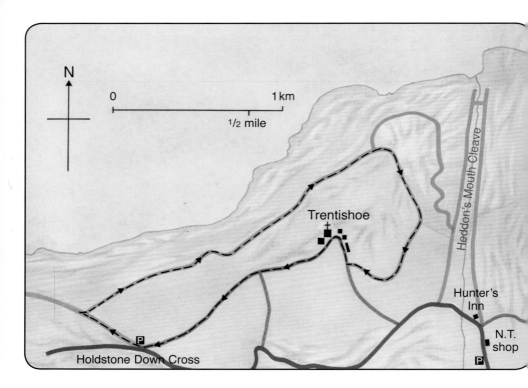

N

0   1 km

1/2 mile

Trentishoe

Heddon's Mouth Cleave

Hunter's
Inn

N.T.
shop

Holdstone Down Cross

Walk 2 Trentishoe

Distance: 5.8km (3 1/2 miles)
*Character: Choose a clear day for this exhilarating walk and
don't forget to take a camera to capture the dramatic views of
Exmoor's unparalleled coastal scenery, including the highest cliffs
in southern Britain. Equally impressive are the bird's eye views
deep into Heddon Valley and Heddon's Mouth Cleave on the
return leg. It is a little longer than other routes in this book, and
there are several ascents and descents, but none are arduous.*

Park on the seaward side of the road opposite Holdstone Down
Cross (SS635479). Facing the sea, take the grassy path downhill
with the fence on your right to the Coastpath.

Turn right on COASTPATH HUNTER'S INN and follow it downhill.
Continue east along the Coastpath to a junction. Fork right
(TRENTISHOE CHURCH), leaving the Coastpath. Keep the fence on
your right.

6

The path soon begins to descend, steeply at first and then more gently. Deep in the Heddon Valley, Heddon's Mouth and its rocky beach come into view and – looking tiny from this height – Hunter's Inn further up the valley.

Continue on the path, which veers south-west, then round to north-west. Reaching a tarred lane, turn right, TRENTISHOE CHURCH.

The lane climbs steeply to the church, which has a list of rectors stretching back to 1260 and a now rare musicians' gallery. Continue uphill on the lane, which begins to level out. Ignore the lane on the left and continue to the start.

Heddon's Mouth
There is a very straightforward walk from Hunter's Inn (National Trust shop, refreshments, toilets, car park) following either side of the river down to the beach at Heddon's Mouth.

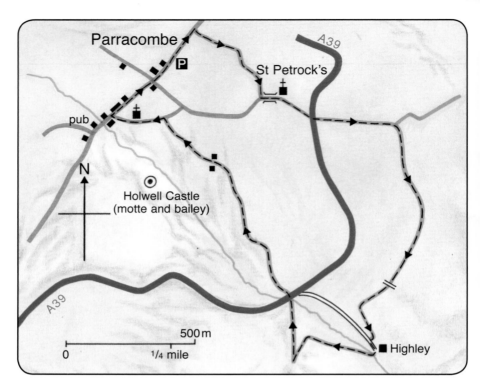

Walk 3   Parracombe

Distance: 4.5km (2³/₄ miles)
Character: A pleasant and fairly gentle walk by field paths,
tracks and lanes, including a medieval church with a remarkable
Georgian interior and a Norman motte and bailey castle.

Start from Parracombe's car park – or park considerately in the
village if this is full. Turn right up the lane for 220m. Turn right
(PUBLIC FOOTPATH) and follow the walled lane for 450m.

Turn left, PUBLIC BRIDLEWAY A39. Cross the old railway bridge,
part of the narrow gauge Lynton & Barnstaple Railway. Divert
left to visit St Petrock's. Continue uphill to the A39, cross carefully and continue uphill PUBLIC BRIDLEWAY PARRACOMBE COMMON.

At the path junction, turn right (PUBLIC FOOTPATH HIGHLEY)
along an enclosed track. Continue ahead when the track ends.
Keeping the hedge on your right, cross a track and continue
ahead (PUBLIC FOOTPATH), keeping the hedge on your right.

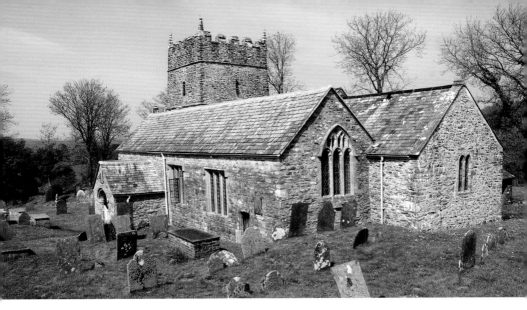

Meeting a track, turn left steeply downhill, FOOTPATH. At Highley, turn left, FOOTPATH. Cross a brook and turn right, PUBLIC FOOTPATH. Follow the track ahead gently uphill to gates. Turn right (FOOTPATH) and left (FOOTPATH) at the end of the field. Cut diagonally left down to a stile. Cross and turn right down the track, BRIDLEWAY. Cross a brook and walk up to the next fingerpost. Turn left, BRIDLEWAY.

Cross the A39. Follow PUBLIC FOOTPATH PARRACOMBE across a field and over the old railway embankment. Cross another field and continue up an enclosed lane for 50 m. Continue with the hedge on your right into another enclosed lane to a farmyard.

Continue for 50 m. Turn left, PUBLIC FOOTPATH PARRACOMBE. Look left to Holwell, a fine example of an early Norman castle. Its motte ditch is partly cut through rock, making it particularly deep and strong. The first Norman castles were built quickly. Earthen ramparts and wooden pallisades formed the 'bailey' or outer defences, protecting a wooden keep on its raised mound.

Cross the field diagonally left as signed. Cross a brook and a stile. Turn left down the lane past Christ Church to a lane junction. Turn right and follow the lane uphill over the crossroads to the car park – or divert left to the Fox and Goose.

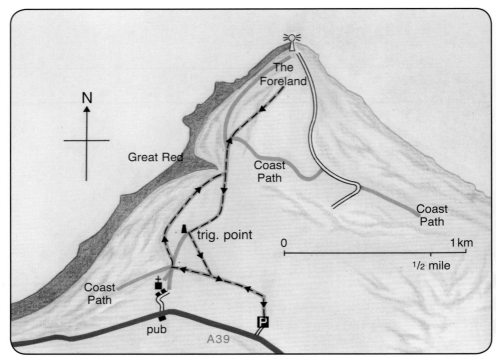

Walk 4 Countisbury and the Foreland

Distance: 3.8 km (2 1/4 miles)

Character: Choose a clear day: the views are stunning, along the coast both east and west and inland across Exmoor. The whole route is on footpaths. There is one short, steep ascent. Listen for skylarks.

Start from the National Trust car park at Barna Barrow, 700 m up the A39 from the Blue Ball Inn (SS753497).

Take the track leading out of the car park with the wall on your left. Turn left at the corner of the wall and continue with the wall on your left to a fingerpost. You may want to divert left here to visit Countisbury church and/or the medieval Blue Ball Inn, which has been dated to around 1300 by its cavernous fireplace, complete with bread oven and cooking jacks.

Otherwise, turn right, COAST PATH. The path is nearly level and well defined, following the contour, with great views west to Lynton and Lynmouth.

At the next fingerpost by Great Red – a huge vertiginous gully of red sandstone formed by a landslip – continue ahead COAST PATH PORLOCK. The path descends to a fingerpost and junction. Bear right and uphill to the highest point of the Foreland, along a rough path. This may be safely followed to the point where the cliff starts to descend steeply.

Now retrace your steps past the last fingerpost to the fingerpost at Great Red. Continue ahead and uphill (COUNTY ROAD), keeping the wall on your left.

On reaching the wall corner, fork right and uphill to the transmitter mast and triangulation pillar (trig. point) on Butter Hill. Fork left on a grassy path to meet a stone wall. Turn left and retrace your steps to the car park.

Warning: There is a path, shown on the map, leading out to the lighthouse. Unfortunately this is a dangerous route even in good weather, so we do not recommend it.

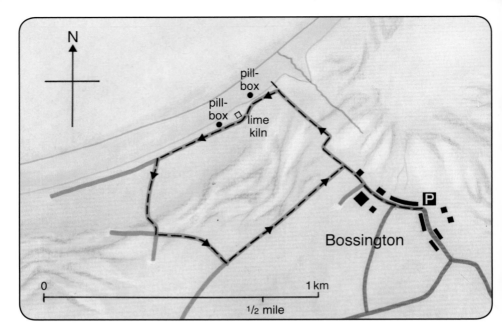

Walk 5 Bossington

Distance: 3.25 km (2 miles)
Character: Bossington is one of Exmoor's most attractive villages.
This easy, level walk by footpaths and quiet lanes includes
sweeping views over Porlock Bay to Exmoor's huge hog-backed
cliffs. Please note, this route crosses marsh, and should be
avoided during very high tides and after heavy rain.

Turn right out of Bossington's National Trust car park, COAST
PATH BOSSINGTON BEACH. Keep right at Myrtle Cottage. Follow
the tarred lane to a path junction. Continue ahead, COAST PATH
PORLOCK WEIR. Stay on the same course at the next fingerpost,
FOOTPATH BEACH. A great view opens out west across the bay.

Continue to the pebble ridge above the beach for superb
views. On your left is a Second World War infantry pillbox.

Retrace your steps for 30 m. Turn right and follow the path
behind the pebble ridge and a ruined lime kiln. Limestone was
shipped onto many West Country beaches and burned in stone-
built kilns to produce agricultural lime for dressing acid soils.

Continue through a kissing gate and over a stile behind a

second pillbox, where a board explains the environmental work that has been done on the salt marsh to improve it as a habitat for wildlife.

Follow the path ahead with the stone wall on your right to another kissing gate. Fork left and keep the wire fence on your left as you head south towards Porlock over marshy ground. Cross two footbridges to reach a path junction.

Turn left (COAST PATH BOSSINGTON) and continue ahead with the salt marsh on your left and fields on your right. Turn left at the next fingerpost, COAST PATH BOSSINGTON. Continue ahead (COASTPATH) between hedges and through a gate, COASTPATH.

Reaching a fingerpost, turn right (BOSSINGTON MINEHEAD) and retrace your steps to the car park.

> Built using beach pebbles, the Bossington pillboxes were garrisoned by up to eight men armed with rifles, light machine guns or anti-tank rifles. They were part of the 'Taunton Stop Line', which ran from the Somerset coast southwards to Seaton in East Devon. It was designed to delay any seaborne German attack further west.

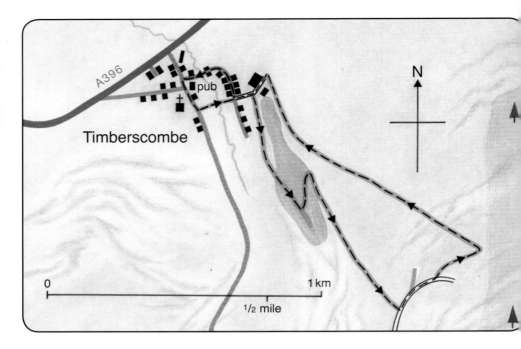

Walk 6 Timberscombe

Distance: 3.5 km (2¹/₄ miles)
Character: Starting from Timberscombe, one of Exmoor's prettiest red sandstone villages, this walk climbs steadily to Timberscombe Common: the views of Dunkery Hill, Dunkery Beacon and down to the sea are superb. The whole walk is on paths, tracks and quiet village streets. There is one long ascent and descent.

Park considerately in the centre of Timberscombe. Facing the Lion Inn, turn right up CHURCH STREET. Walk past the parish churchyard. Turn left, PUBLIC FOOTPATH. Walk down steps past the Methodist Church, to a stream and uphill to a lane. Continue up the lane for 60 m. Turn right, PUBLIC BRIDLEWAY TIMBERSCOMBE COMMON. Follow the rough track uphill past a modern house and through a wooden gate.

Continue as the track climbs steadily to woodland. Turn left, BRIDLEWAY. Follow the track steeply uphill. It doglegs right. Follow it uphill through gates and on to a second pair of gates.

14

Turn left, BRIDLEWAY. The path forks almost immediately. Keep right and uphill along a vehicle track. When this veers hard right, leave it and walk ahead to a wooden gate. Bear slightly right across the next field to a woodland gate.

Turn left, BRIDLEWAY TIMBERSCOMBE. Follow the path gently downhill. Continue downhill (TIMBERSCOMBE) at the next gate. At the gate after that, continue ahead with the woodland on your left to stables. Reaching the gate below the stables, turn left.

Walk downhill to the crossroads and turn right into GREAT HOUSE STREET. Follow it round to the Lion Inn.

St Petrock's Church is constructed of attractive local red sandstone. Most of it is 15th century, including the south door, with its splendid ironwork. When the north door was uncovered in 1955 the mural painting above it of King David was revealed. The church has many other beautiful features, including the fan-vaulted screen, made around 1500.

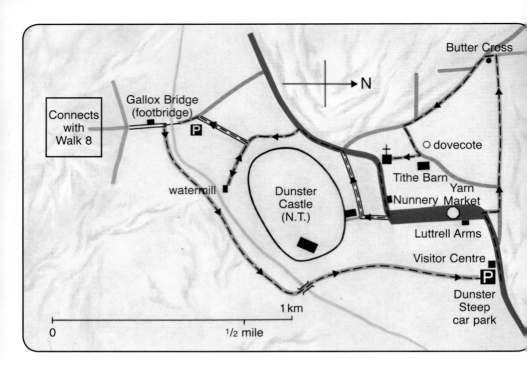

Walk 7   Around Dunster

Distance: 3.1km (2 miles)

Character: This short walk is packed with interest and historic buildings, including Dunster's Castle and 15th century church, the Yarn Market (1589), the Luttrell Arms, the Butter Cross, tithe barn and dovecote – all medieval. As well as its extraordinarily rich heritage of historic buildings, Dunster enjoys a beautiful setting between wooded hills and the sea.

Leave the top end of Dunster Steep car park past the National Park Visitor Centre, which has tableaux explaining Exmoor life and a range of local books and maps. Follow the main street past the Luttrell Arms to the polygonal Yarn Market.

Retrace your steps for 30m and continue up a short footpath. Turn left. Continue ahead, PUBLIC FOOTPATH BUTTER CROSS. The path follows a tarmac drive through a kissing gate into a broad grassy path leading to the Butter Cross. Turn left down ST GEORGE'S STREET.

Turn left into PRIORY GREEN. Walk through an arch to see the dovecote and the well restored tithe barn.

Turn right through the memorial garden to enter the church by the north door. Leave by the south porch. Turn left down Church Street (beware of traffic) and turn right opposite the slate-hung medieval Nunnery through a gate marked DUNSTER CASTLE AND GARDENS. Walk uphill to the ticket office. Either visit the Castle now, or bear right past the toilets and downhill.

Turn left into WEST STREET and follow the cobbled pavement past a pleasing medley of historic buildings, including the medieval Stag's Head. Turn left along MILL LANE. Walk with the leat on your left to the Water Mill.

Retrace your steps for 75 m. Turn left into an alley and turn left again to cross Gallox Bridge (see page 18). Turn almost immediately left (PERMITTED FOOTPATH FOLLOWS RIVER). Continue past the mill, the castle gardens and a charming 18th century bridge. Cross the river by a second stone bridge. Turn right (PERMITTED PATH DUNSTER STEEP) and follow it as it curves left to a lane.

Cross the lane. Go through the gate and car park in front of you to a second gate. Follow the grassy path ahead to the start.

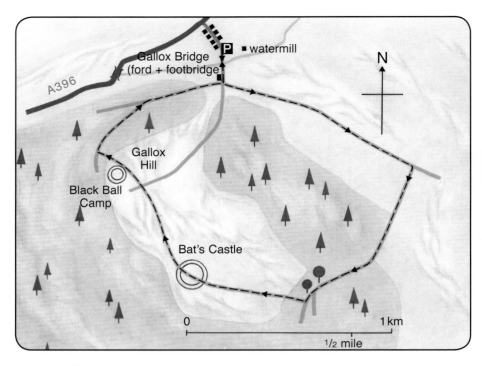

Walk 8   Dunster to Bat's Castle

Distance: 4.4 km (2³/4 miles)
Character: As well as splendid views of Exmoor, the coast and Dunster Castle, this walk includes two well preserved Iron Age camps and a charming packhorse bridge.

Start from the small car park on Park Street at the southern end of Dunster, off West Street. Turn left and walk past thatched cottages. Cross Gallox Bridge and continue ahead, DUNSTER FOREST CROWN ESTATE. Walk past thatched cottages to a fingerpost.

Turn left, CARHAMPTON WITHYCOMBE. Keep left at the next fingerpost, FOOTPATH CARHAMPTON. Follow the broad grassy path ahead through fields and a gate. Enjoy the views of Dunster Castle. Continue over grass to a second gate.

Turn right (WITHYCOMBE HILL GATE) and follow the rough track uphill. To the east there are fine views of the Quantock hills and the coast. Continue uphill through trees. When the track forks, keep right and uphill through a beech avenue to the next

18

fingerpost, BRIDLEWAY TO DUNSTER. Continue ahead, PERMITTED FOOTPATH BAT'S CASTLE. At the next path junction, continue ahead (BAT'S CASTLE CIRCUIT) into Bat's Castle, where there is an explanatory information board.

Leave the castle by a broad grassy path downhill. Continue ahead at the next fingerpost, BAT'S CASTLE CIRCUIT. The track forks. Keep left and follow the broad grassy track around the rim of Black Ball camp. Continue downhill to a path junction.

Turn right (BAT'S CASTLE CIRCUIT) and follow the path downhill to another path junction. Turn right, DUNSTER. Follow the track downhill and retrace your steps over Gallox Bridge to the start.

> **Bat's Castle** is an Iron Age camp, built between 400 and 100 BC. The castle's two ramparts of stone and earth are over 4 m high in parts and were dug from a deep ditch lying between them. At 213 m above sea level it gives panoramic views – once probably a defensive necessity, now a pleasure for visitors. Nearby Black Ball camp on Gallox Hill is also Iron Age and a little smaller in diameter, with a 3 m high rampart and a 2 m deep ditch.

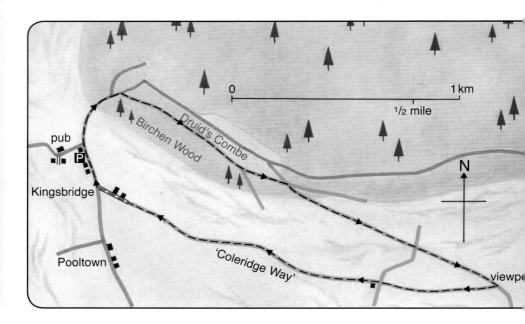

Walk 9 Luxborough and Druid's Combe

Distance: 4.3km (2³/₄ miles)
Character: Starting from the pretty Brendon village of
Luxborough, with its red sandstone and thatched buildings, this
route climbs wooded Druid's Combe to an airy hilltop with fine
views of the coast and across the green Brendon patchwork to
Dunkery. Mainly off road, there is one steady ascent and descent.

Turn left out of the car park at Kingsbridge, Luxborough. Walk
past the lane junction – noticing the Royal Oak to the left, a
charming stone built inn with low beamed ceilings, slate flagged
floor, log fire and beer garden.

When the lane forks, continue ahead (ROADWATER WASHFORD)
for 70m. Turn right, PUBLIC FOOTPATH TREBOROUGH. Follow the
broad stony track through woodland. Ignore side turnings.
When the track forks, keep ahead (left).

Continue to a footpath junction. Bear right, FOOTPATH. Follow
the footpath uphill through trees to a stile. Walk ahead through
the field with the hedge on your right. Leave the field by a gate
at the far top corner.

20

Continue ahead on the same course diagonally left across the next field to the rocky summit of the hill – a superb viewpoint.

The field gate just beyond the summit is marked with a yellow post and a quill pen symbol for the Coleridge Way. This long distance path, part of which you follow to Luxborough, was named in honour of poet Samuel Taylor Coleridge who lived for a short but productive period at Nether Stowey, in the Quantock hills, near his friends William and Dorothy Wordsworth. All three loved walking and roamed the countryside with enthusiasm.

Do not go through the gate. Turn right and walk ahead (west) with the hedge on your left. Leave the field at the far end by a steel gate. Continue on the same course through another steel gate and on through the next field, which has an interesting medley of old farm machinery. Leave by a gate just to the right of farm buildings. Continue ahead, BRIDLEWAY LUXBOROUGH.

Go through a gate and continue with the hedge on your right to the next gate. Walk ahead on the enclosed track through a series of gates to a house. Follow the tarmac track down to the car park.

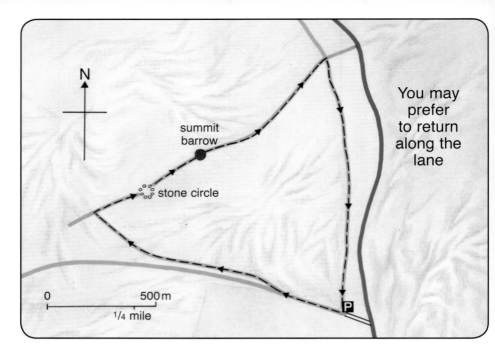

Walk 10 Withypool Hill

Distance: 3.1 km (2 miles)
Character: This gentle walk to the summit of Withypool Hill
(398 m) is rewarded with panoramic views. Crowned with a
prehistoric barrow (burial mound), Withypool Hill has one of
Exmoor's best stone circles. Both circle and barrow date from the
Bronze Age.

Park off-road near the cattle grid, 1.5 km (1 mile) south of Withypool on the lane to Hawkridge (SS 847338). Walk ahead (PUBLIC BRIDLEWAY WITHYPOOL) with the hedgebank on your left.

The track divides. Keep right, veering slightly away from the hedgebank. The track divides again near the point where the hedgebank takes a 90° turn left. Keep slightly right, and slightly right again at the next division.

Meeting a cross path, turn sharp right and follow it uphill. This path passes through the centre of the stone circle. Although there are at least 37 stones, most are no more than shin-high and the circle itself is easily missed amid the heather, especially in

summer. Look out not only for the stones themselves, but also the circular path through the heather.

Continue on the path uphill to the summit barrow. Some 25 metres in diameter, with a stone cairn in the centre, this is one of several prehistoric burial mounds on Exmoor and a magnificent viewpoint. Brightworthy Barrows lie 2 km north-west on Withypool Common, Dunkery 12 km north-east, and Winsford Hill 3 km to the east.

Turn east and follow the well-beaten path. This is level at first and then descends gently to a cross path. Either turn right (south) at this point and follow the rough path back to the start, or continue north-east on the well-beaten path to the lane and turn right (south) to follow the lane back to the start.

Because ponies have made their own tracks hereabouts, following the rough path means picking your way carefully through long grass, gorse and heather – so boots and long trousers are needed!

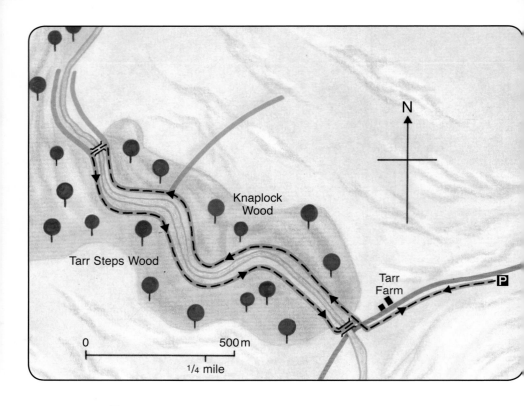

Walk 11   Tarr Steps

Distance: 3.2 km (2 miles)
Character: A delightful bankside walk beside the river Barle
from Tarr Steps, one of Exmoor's most intriguing historic sites.
One short, steepish ascent and some uneven footing.

Follow the footpath (not the lane) downhill from Tarr Steps car park to Tarr Steps. Turn right and follow the east bank of the Barle upriver, PUBLIC BRIDLEWAY WITHYPOOL. Continue beyond the bridlepath for Knaplock for 300m to a footbridge.

   Cross the river and turn left, BRIDLEWAY TARR STEPS VIA FORD. As a walker you won't have to use the ford! Simply follow the bankside path to Tarr Steps. Cross the river and either divert immediately left to 16th century Tarr Farm (now an inn and restaurant) for refreshments, or retrace your steps directly to the car park.

Tarr Steps

Consisting of seventeen slabs of flat stone, each weighing up to two tonnes and over two metres long, Tarr Steps is 55 m from end to end, and would be an impressive engineering feat if constructed today with modern machinery.

Indeed, it underwent substantial repairs in 1942 and 1979, and most notably when it was largely reconstructed by Royal Engineers after the terrible Exmoor floods of August 1952. That deluge claimed 34 lives at Lynmouth and wreaked havoc with moorland bridges, after more than 225 mm (9 inches) of rain pounded high Exmoor in just two days.

The origin of Tarr Steps has been much debated. Most authorities now agree this magnificent Grade 1 listed clapper bridge is medieval, not older than the 13th century. However, the neighbouring ford may have been part of a much older trackway.

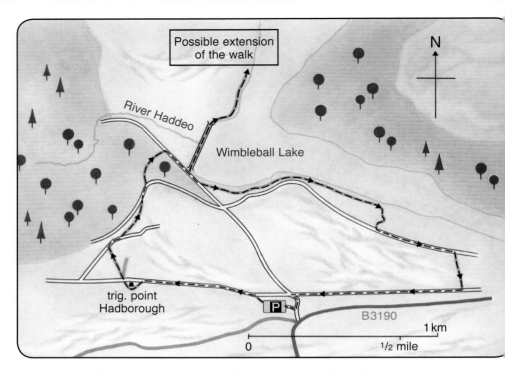

Walk 12 Haddon Hill and Wimbleball

Distance: 4.7 km (3 miles)

Character: As well as panoramic views, there is a pleasant mix of heather moorland, woodland and lakeside paths with one longish descent and ascent. There are so many paths on Haddon Hill, some created by the hill's Exmoor pony herd, that extra attention to map and directions are needed.

Start from the signed car park on Haddon Hill. With your back to the information board and toilets, walk to the far end of the car park. Leave by the gate on the right. Follow the well-beaten track to the summit of Hadborough Hill ahead. A slight diversion left leads to the triangulation pillar and superb views.

Walk back to the main track. Cross it and take the path ahead, indicated by a row of stumpy wooden posts. The path immediately divides. Fork left and follow the path gently downhill through heather and bracken to a cross track. Turn right and follow this downhill for only 50 m. Branch left onto a rough path

leading downhill to join a vehicle track. Turn right and follow this downhill for only 40 m.

Look out for a fingerpost on your left, partly hidden by branches. Turn left, FOOTPATH TO HARTFORD. Follow the footpath over a stile and downhill through trees to a concrete track. Turn right, BRIDLEWAY TO UPTON. Follow the track uphill to a fingerpost at the end of the dam.

You may wish to divert left across the dam to enjoy the view or explore the far bank. Otherwise, bear left, UPTON VIA RESERVOIR. Continue along the bankside path (part of a 14.5 km path circuiting the lake) to a footbridge. Cross and continue along the bank for 400 m until the path veers away from the bank at a water inlet.

Walk only 20 m uphill. Bear right through a seven barred wooden gate. Follow the path diagonally right and uphill to a cross track. Turn right, then left at the next junction.

Continue steadily up the track for 400 m. Turn right and take the left of two paths steeply uphill to the next junction. Turn right and follow the level track for 900 m. Meeting a tarmac track, turn left and then next right through a gate to the car park.

There-and-back walks

Walk 13   Chains Barrow and Pinkworthy ('Pinkery') Pond

This 7 km (4¹/₂ mile) walk gives sweeping moorland views. It climbs steadily to Exmoor's high watershed, 487 m above sea level, on Chains Barrow, a prehistoric burial chamber capped by a triangulation pillar. It then follows a level route to Pinkery Pond, a 3 ha (7 acre) lake, dug at the headwaters of the river Barle in the early 19th century at the behest of pioneering Exmoor landowner John Knight for reasons unknown. Possibly, it was to power mining machinery, maybe it was simply to create an impressive landscape feature.

Park in the parking area beside the B3358 at SS729401. From the eastern (Simonsbath) end follow BRIDLEWAY CHAINS BARROW. Keeping the wall on your right, follow the blue markers across two fields. Continue through the wooden gate on the same course, using blue marker posts to guide you (some had fallen at the time of writing). At a path junction, go through a gate, bear right, and walk on for 330 m to CHAINS BARROW. Retrace your steps to the path junction. Turn right, PINKERY POND. Keep the fence on your right up to a gate; then walk on with the fence on your left.

Birchcleave Wood, a mature beech wood of particular charm in spring and autumn

The site of Wheal Eliza. As with many other Exmoor enterprises, this mine was the work of entrepreneurs John and Frederic Knight. Looking for copper, they found only unprofitable quantities of iron ore and the mine closed in 1857

Walk 14   Simonsbath and Wheal Eliza

This gentle route follows the river Barle from Simonsbath to Wheal Eliza, a distance of 2 km (1 1/4 miles).

Start from the signed car park in Simonsbath. Walk back to the road and turn right. At the foot of the slope, turn left onto the Two Moors Way for COW CASTLE PICKED STONES. After 20 m, bear right, COW CASTLE.

Follow the well-beaten path through Birchcleave Wood. Continue along the valley, behind Flexbarrow and on to the spoil heap and ruined cottages at Wheal Eliza.

Walk 15 Doone Valley

This delightful and easy bankside walk along Badgeworthy Water explores 'Doone Valley', the setting for R D Blackmore's swashbuckling Exmoor novel, *Lorna Doone* (1869).

Start from the car park behind Lorna Doone Farm (gift shop and refreshments). This was probably the model for Plover's Barrow Farm, home of the novel's hero, Jan Ridd. Go through the gate ahead and follow the path (modest entrance charge) along the west bank for 1 km to Clouds Farm – where more refreshments are offered. The path may be followed for a further 2.5 km to an abandoned medieval village, containing the ruins of typical medieval longhouses, which had one room for the farmer and his family and one for the animals.

Walk 16 Selworthy Beacon and Bossington Hill

Park on the right of Hill Road (accessed from Higher Town, Minehead) at SS 927476. Walk west along Hill Road for 350 m to the sign BRIDLEWAY SELWORTHY BEACON. Continue for another 150 m. Turn right up a stony track (NO UNAUTHORIZED VEHICLES)

Right: Exmoor mare and foal on Dunkery Beacon

Opposite: The River Barle in 'Doone Valley'

to Selworthy Beacon. At 380m, this is a magnificent viewpoint overlooking Dunkery, the Exmoor coast and South Wales. Do not divert left to the lane, but walk ahead on the broad ridge track, which is joined by the Coast Path. When the track divides, fork left (BOSSINGTON & LYNCH) for a superb vista of Porlock Bay.

Walk 17 Allerford and Selworthy

This walk includes two of Exmoor's most attractive villages. Turn right out of Allerford car park. Only 50m ahead, turn left over the 17th century packhorse bridge. Follow the lane ahead. It curves right, but when it curves right again by a thatched cottage, walk straight ahead up a stony track to Selworthy. Reaching the village, turn left past the 14th century tithe barn and left through a brown wooden gate to the tearooms and National Trust Information Centre/Shop. Continue up the path to the historic limewashed church.

Walk 18 Dunkery Beacon

Dunkery Beacon is signed from the B3224 Exford/Wheddon Cross road. Park by the small bridge at Dunkery Gate, SS896406. Walk 50m up the lane. Turn left and follow PUBLIC BRIDLEWAY DUNKERY BEACON for 1.1km (3/4 mile) to the summit. At 519m (1713ft) this is the highest hill on Exmoor and a marvellous viewpoint.

Walk 19   Winsford Punchbowl

Leave your car in the parking area on the eastern side of the B3223 1km (½ mile) north of Spire Cross, SS878342. Simply follow PUBLIC BRIDLEWAY HALSE LANE for 300m to the rim of the Punchbowl. A dramatic natural amphitheatre, the Punchbowl opens out onto a splendid view to Dunkery Beacon, the highest point on Exmoor.

Some other Bossiney books you may find useful

Shortish Walks on Exmoor (6-9km)
Exmoor Pub Walks (8-15km)
Exmoor – A Shortish Guide
Lynton and Lynmouth – A Shortish Guide
The Somerset Coast: Beaches and Walks
Devon Beach and Cove Guide
Really Short Walks North Devon (3-5km)
Shortish Walks North Devon (5-9km)

For a full list of our walks and guide books covering Somerset, Devon and Cornwall, please see our website www.bossineybooks.com